Mon in the Ferns

By Sally Cowan

Mon and Kip lazed
in the ferns.

They were snacking on bugs
and herbs.

"The sky looks dark up there," said Kip.

"Mum will be stern if I get wet!" said Mon.
"Let's take the herbs home."

But as Mon picked herbs,
he felt a poke from a big bill!

"Oh, a bird!" he yelled.

He jerked his hand away.

"Sorry!" said the tern.
"But have you seen my chick?
She is very fluffy,
and she cheeps a lot!"

"No," said Mon.

"She is not in the ferns."

"And she is not in the herbs,"
Kip added.

"Is she in your nest?"
said Mon.

"No, she is not in my nest!"
said the tern.

"Perk up!" said Mon.
"We will find her!"

Mon and Kip left the ferns
and swung up on a long vine.

Mon swerved on his vine
and looked up.

The tern's chick was high up
in a tree.

"It's your chick!" yelled Mon.

Cheep! Cheep!

The tern looked up.

"Thank you!" she yelled.

Then, big rain drops fell.

Mon and Kip got soaked!

At home, Mum was stern.

"You are wet!" she said.

"But we helped a tern
find her chick!" said Mon.
"And I got you some
sweet herbs!"

"Well, that **was** kind," said Mum.

And she served Mon herbs for tea.

CHECKING FOR MEANING

1. Who do Mon and Kip help? *(Literal)*

2. What did Mon bring home for Mum? *(Literal)*

3. Why might Mum have been cross that Mon got wet? *(Inferential)*

EXTENDING VOCABULARY

stern	What does Mon mean when he says, *"Mum will be stern if I get wet!"*? What other word could Mon have used instead of *stern*?
tern	What do you know about what a *tern* is from reading the book? What questions do you have about terns?
swerved	What would it have looked like when Mon *swerved* on his vine? What else can swerve?

MOVING BEYOND THE TEXT

1. What else do monkeys like to eat?

2. What kinds of herbs have you tried?

3. What are some other types of birds besides terns?

4. How could you be kind like Mon?

SPEED SOUNDS

ar	er	ir	ur	or

PRACTICE WORDS

ferns

herbs

bird

jerked

stern

tern

Perk

dark

swerved

tern's

her

served